The Kids Hymns Project

An exciting new worship experience for children

Featuring 15 hymns and their stories

Created by Pam Andrews

Arranged in a rockin' Praise and Worship style by

Steven V. Taylor

LILLENAS
PUBLISHING COMPANY

lillenas.com

Contents

The Solid Rock

Hymn writer: Edward Mote (1797-1874)
Composer: William B. Bradbury (1816-1868)

Scripture Reference: 1 Corinthians 3:11 *"For no one can lay any foundation other than the one already laid, which is Jesus Christ."* (NIV)

"The Solid Rock" reminds us to build our lives on the Rock of Jesus Christ. It was written by Edward Mote, who was born in London, England on January 21, 1797. His home life was very sad. His parents were poor and did not teach him about Jesus. He often spent his days walking the streets. As he grew, he finally became an apprentice to a cabinetmaker. When he was 16 years old, the cabinetmaker took him to hear John Hyatt, a fine preacher. At that church meeting, Mote became a Christian.

A visit to a dying woman inspired Mote to write "The Solid Rock." Mote always liked to sing a hymn at the end of every visit to a sick friend. On this day, he realized he had forgotten his hymnal. He had written the poem "The Solid Rock" earlier and had it in his pocket. He shared the poem with the lady. The poem was later published.

Later in life, Mote helped build a church in Horsham, Sussex, England. He preached there until he had to retire due to health problems. He died November 13, 1874.

William B. Bradbury composed music to "The Solid Rock." William Bradbury was one of the finest Christian composers of his time.

(Remember, when we refer to the "hymn" we are referring to the words. The music is called the "hymn tune.")

The Solid Rock

EDWARD MOTE

WILLIAM B. BRADBURY
Arranged by Steven V. Taylor

CD: 5

Solo
f

When

Rock, I __ stand. __ Yeah, __   yeah, __

F2/A   F/A   C2

36

He shall __ come with trum - pet __ sound, O

C2   G

may I __ then in Him be __ found! Dressed

F   C sus/G   C

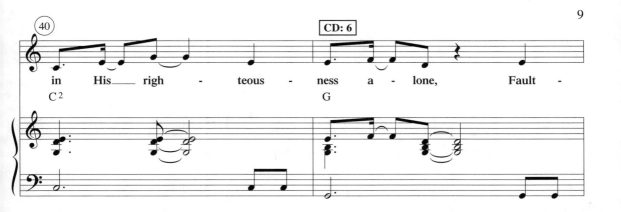

in His___ righ - teous - ness a - lone, Fault -

C²   G

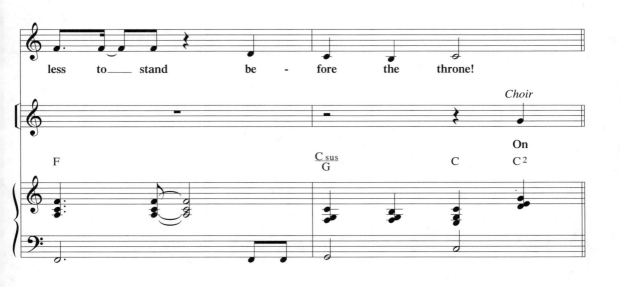

less to__ stand be - fore the throne!

Choir

On

F   Csus/G   C   C²

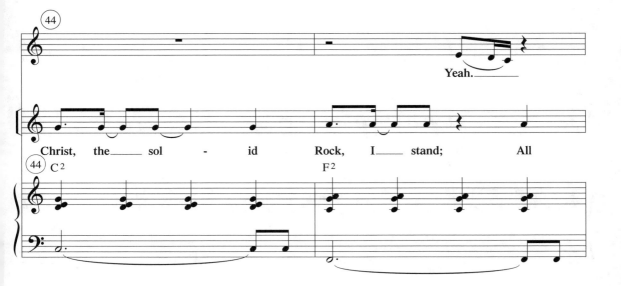

Christ, the__ sol - id Rock, I__ stand; All

Yeah.__

C²   F²

When I Survey the Wondrous Cross

Hymn writer: Isaac Watts (1674-1748)
Composer: Gregorian Chant, adapted by Lowell Mason (1792-1872)

Scripture Reference: John 19:17 *"Carrying his own cross, he went out to the place of the Skull (which in Aramaic is called Golgotha)."* (NIV)

"When I Survey the Wondrous Cross" is one of the favorite hymns we sing during the Lenten season. This hymn tells the story of the crucifixion in such a way that it brings the scene to life. The writer of this hymn was Isaac Watts. He was born on July 17, 1674 in South Hampton, England. He was very smart. He learned Latin when he was 5, Greek when he was 9, French when he was 11, and Hebrew when he was 13. The Christian hymns during this time were not appealing to Isaac, so much so that he complained to his father. His father encouraged him to write his own hymns. He began that night, and would try to write a new hymn each week. Hymn writing was a way he could express himself. "When I Survey the Wondrous Cross" was written in 1707 for a communion service. This hymn expresses the strong feelings within his heart about the sacrifice Christ made for us on the cross.

The tune of this hymn was Lowell Mason's adaptation of a Gregorian chant. Lowell Mason made a huge contribution to Christian music. In fact, he is known as the "father of American church music."

(Remember, when we refer to the "hymn" we are referring to the words. The music is called the "hymn tune").

When I Survey the Wondrous Cross

ISAAC WATTS

LOWELL MASON
Arranged by Steven V. Taylor

14

3. See, from His head, His hands, His feet,

D²   D sus   D²

Sor - row and love flow min - gled down.

D²   B m   C²

Did e'er such love and sor - row meet,

C²   D²   D sus   D²

CD: 10

Or thorns com - pose so rich a

B m   A/C#   G   A sus   A²

Holy, Holy, Holy! Lord God Almighty

Hymn writer: Reginald Heber (1783-1826)
Composer: John B. Dykes (1823-1876)

Scripture Reference: Psalm 95:6-7 *"Come, let us bow down in worship, let us kneel before the LORD our Maker; for he is our God and we are the people of his pasture, the flock under his care."* (NIV)

"Holy, Holy, Holy! Lord God Almighty" is a hymn that is one of the most popular praise hymns of all time. It reminds us to give our praise to God, the Three in One.

Reginald Heber was born on April 21, 1783 in Cheshire, England. His family had a prominent position in their community and was well educated. When Heber was seventeen, he began his studies at Oxford University. He was a very good student. He then became a minister in a small church in England. He was a fine leader and was known for his integrity throughout his ministry. He also was known for his hymns and poetry. Later in his life he went to India to continue his work for the Lord. This job was difficult and caused Heber to be in poor health. He died three years after arriving in India. "Holy, Holy, Holy! Lord God Almighty" was written to honor God the Father, God the Son, and God the Holy Spirit.

The music for "Holy, Holy, Holy! Lord God Almighty" was written by Dr. John B. Dykes. Dykes played many musical instruments and was a church organist at age 12. He was also a leading composer during his time. In fact, he wrote over 300 melodies for hymns, many still in use today.

(Remember, when we refer to the "hymn" we are referring to the words. The music is called the "hymn tune").

Holy, Holy, Holy! Lord God Almighty

REGINALD HEBER

JOHN B. DYKES
Arranged by Steven V. Taylor

God in three Per - sons,_____ bless - ed Trin - i -
Per - fect in pow'r, in_____ love, in pu - ri -

E♭2   G m7   C m7   F

1 f   26 CD: 14   (to pg. 21, meas. 9)

ty!
B♭2   A♭/B♭   E♭/B♭   B♭

2 f   CD: 16

ty!
B♭2   A♭/B♭   E♭/B♭

33

Lord You're ho - ly, You're ho - ly, You're

B♭   B♭2   A♭/B♭

CD: 18

earth, and sky, and sea.

D sus   D   G

50 Choir

Ho - ly, ho - ly, ho - ly!_____ mer-ci-ful and

C 2   G/C   F/A

54

might - y!_____ God in three Per - sons,_____

C/G   F 2   A m7

bless - ed Trin - i - ty!

D m7   G   C 2

Wonderful Words of Life

Hymn writer and Composer: Philip P. Bliss (1838-1876)

Scripture Reference: Hebrews 4:12 *"For the word of God is living and active. Sharper than any double edged sword, it penetrates even to dividing soul and spirit, joints and marrow; it judges the thoughts and attitudes of the heart."* (NIV)

The Word of God is our guide for life. The Bible has an amazing healing quality. When you are afraid, the words will comfort you. When you need guidance, the words will lead you. When you feel hopeless, the words will give you hope. The Word of God is our guide for life. If we will follow these teachings, our life on earth will be happier and more joyful. We are reminded of this every time we sing "Wonderful Words of Life."

Philip P. Bliss wrote this hymn as well as many others. Bliss was born July 9, 1838, in Clearfield County, Pennsylvania. He grew up poor. He asked Jesus in his heart when he was 12 years old. For many years he traveled with famous evangelists like D. L. Moody to help lead revivals. Bliss was a fine singer and conductor. Sadly, on one of his revival trips at the age of 38, Bliss and his wife were involved in a deadly train accident. While his wife lost her life in the accident, Bliss lived long enough to attempt to rescue her. He perished in his effort as the train caught fire.

The tune to "Wonderful Words of Life" was also written by Philip Bliss. Because Bliss was such a fine musician, he was able to compose music as well as write lyrics. Many of the hymns composed by Bliss are still sung today in local churches.

(Remember, when we refer to the "hymn" we are referring to the words. The music is called the "hymn tune").

Wonderful Words of Life

Words and Music by
PHILIP P. BLISS
Arranged by Steven V. Taylor

34

All Hail the Power of Jesus' Name

Hymn writer: Edward Perronet (1726-1792)
Composer: Oliver Holden (1765-1844)

Scripture Reference: Revelation 4:11 *"You are worthy, our Lord and God, to receive glory and honor and power, for you created all things, and by your will they were created and have their being."* (NIV)

If there was ever a hymn written that could reflect the way every Christian should feel, it would certainly be "All Hail the Power of Jesus' Name." Edward Perronet wrote this hymn. Perronet was born in 1726 at Sundridge, Kent, England. His father was a pastor in the State Church of England. Perronet also became a minister, but he did not agree with the ways of the church. He eventually left the church and began supporting the evangelical movement of that time. He was often persecuted for his beliefs. Perronet finally became the pastor of an independent church in Canterbury, England.

"All Hail the Power of Jesus' Name" has been sung with three different tunes. The most popular tune is called "Coronation," which was composed by Oliver Holden. Holden was from Massachusetts and was a carpenter and musician. There is another tune for "All Hail the Power of Jesus' Name" that is popular in Great Britain called "Miles Lane," composed by William Shrubsole, and another called "Diadem," which was composed by James Eller. "All Hail the Power of Jesus' Name" is one of the finest praise and worship hymns ever written.

(Remember, when we refer to the "hymn" we are referring to the words. The music is called the "hymn tune")

All Hail the Power of Jesus' Name

EDWARD PERRONET

OLIVER HOLDEN
Arranged by Steven V. Taylor

Lyrics:

1. All hail the pow'r of Je-sus' name! Let an-gels pros-trate_____ fall. Bring
(2. Ye) cho-sen seed of Is-rael's race, Ye ran-somed from the_____ fall, Hail

CD: 27

(to pg. 36, meas. 9)

2. Ye

40

Blessed Assurance

Hymn writer: Fanny J. Crosby (1820-1915)
Composer: Phoebe Palmer Knapp (1839-1908)

Scripture Reference: Hebrews 10:22 *"...let us draw near to God with a sincere heart in full assurance of faith, having our hearts sprinkled to cleanse us from a guilty conscience and having our bodies washed with pure water."* (NIV)

"Blessed Assurance" was written Fanny Jane Crosby, who is considered to be one of the best hymn-writers of all time. She was born in Southeast, New York on March 24, 1820. Her parents were simple people. When she was six years old she became blind because of a medical mistake. She was a member of the St. John's Methodist Episcopal Church in New York City and attended the New York School for the Blind. She later became a teacher at the blind school.

Fanny first wrote secular songs that were popular in her day. It was William B. Bradbury, a well-know church musician, who influenced her to begin writing gospel songs. Fanny Crosby was a devout woman of God. It is said that she always prayed for guidance before writing any song. Fanny Crosby wrote over 8000 gospel songs, many of which are still being sung today. Fanny died at the age of 95.

Mrs. Phoebe Palmer Knapp wrote the music to "Blessed Assurance." She played her tune for Fanny Crosby and Fanny immediately knew the words to the song should be "Blessed assurance, Jesus is mine." Mrs. Knapp also wrote many gospel songs. She had over 500 songs published.

(Remember, when we refer to the "hymn" we are referring to the words. The music is called the "hymn tune").

Blessed Assurance

FANNY J. CROSBY

PHOEBE PALMER KNAPP
Arranged by Steven V. Taylor

44

CD: 33

I Surrender All

Hymn writer: Judson W. Van DeVenter (1855-1939)
Composer: Winfield S. Weeden (1847-1908)

Scripture Reference: Matthew 10:39 *"Whoever finds his life will lose it, and whoever loses his life for my sake will find it."* (NIV)

"I Surrender All" reminds us to give control of our hearts and lives to Jesus. Judson Van DeVenter wrote this hymn as he was trying to make a decision about the direction of his life– whether to continue his work in art or to become a minister. Born in Dundee, Michigan, he went to Hillsdale College. After graduation, he became an art teacher. Through the years, though, it was obvious to his friends that Van DeVenter also had an ability to preach. His surrender to the call of ministry helped transform the lives of many.

Winfield S. Weeden worked with Judson Van DeVenter. He was a great singer and conductor. He was born in Middleport, Ohio on March 29, 1847. The pairing of these men by our Lord gave us several marvelous hymns, including "I Surrender All."

(Remember, when we refer to the "hymn" we are referring to the words. The music is called the "hymn tune").

I Surrender All

JUDSON W. VAN DEVENTER

WINFIELD S. WEEDEN
Arranged by Steven V. Taylor

52

CD: 39 / 41
1st / 2nd time

54

My Jesus, I Love Thee

Hymn writer: William R. Featherstone (1846-1873)
Composer: Adoniram J. Gordon (1836-1895)

Scripture Reference: 1 John 4:19 *"We love because he first loved us."* (NIV)

Love songs to Jesus truly must be wonderful for our Lord to hear. It is important to tell our Lord how much we love Him every day. "My Jesus, I Love Thee" is a great hymn of love given to us by William R. Featherstone. What is so amazing about this hymn is that it was written when Featherstone was only 16 years old.

William Featherstone was born in Montreal, Canada on July 23, 1846. It was after his salvation experience that these words came to him. It is thought that William's aunt is responsible for getting this hymn published in "The London Hymn Book." Isn't it glorious that our Lord can use us at any age to accomplish His work? Featherstone proves that a young person can make a real difference in the world.

Dr. A. J. Gordon, a pastor of a church in Boston, Massachusetts, saw Featherstone's hymn in "The London Hymn Book." A new melody came to Dr. Gordon for the poem, giving us the tune we have today. Dr. Gordon was himself a minister, literary editor, editor of a magazine, a musician, and a missionary to India. The Lord showed His great plan by uniting these two talented men to create such a beautiful hymn.

(Remember, when we refer to the "hymn" we are referring to the words. The music is called the "hymn tune").

My Jesus, I Love Thee

WILLIAM R. FEATHERSTONE

ADONIRAM J. GORDON
Arranged by Steven V. Taylor

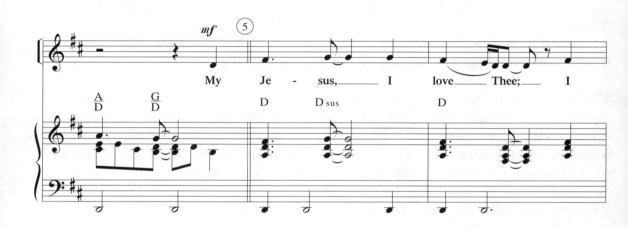

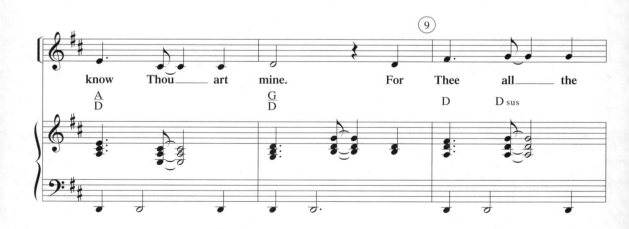

57

58

What a Friend We Have in Jesus

Hymn writer: Joseph Scriven (1819-1886)
Composer: Charles C. Converse (1832-1918)

Scripture Reference: Proverbs 18:24 *"A man of many companions may come to ruin, but there is a friend who sticks closer than a brother."* (NIV)

"What a Friend We Have in Jesus" must certainly be considered to be one of the favorite hymns of all Christians. Joseph Scriven wrote this familiar hymn. Joseph was born in 1819 in Dublin, Ireland, and lived a comfortable life with his parents. At age 25, he decided to move to Canada because he had developed different beliefs, and his bride-to-be had died in a drowning accident. He lived a life of sacrifice, constantly giving to those in need. Scriven wrote "What a Friend We Have in Jesus" as a gift to his ill mother. The poem was noticed by a friend and later published. He died, as had his fiancée, of an accidental drowning.

Charles C. Converse composed the music to "What a Friend We Have in Jesus." He studied classical music in Germany, but became a lawyer after returning to America. Converse continued to write music for the church, as well. The tune of "What a Friend We Have in Jesus" is known throughout the world.

(Remember, when we refer to the "hymn" we are referring to the words. The music is called the "hymn tune").

What a Friend We Have in Jesus

JOSEPH M. SCRIVEN

CHARLES C. CONVERSE
Arranged by Steven V. Taylor

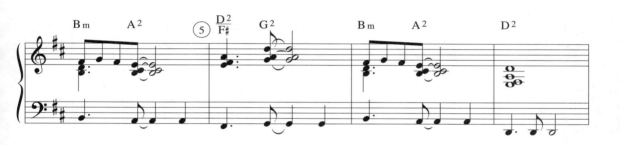

1. What a Friend we have in Je - sus,
2. Have we tri - als and temp - ta - tions?

66

CD: 51

Come, Thou Fount of Every Blessing

Hymn writer: Robert Robinson (1735-1790)
Composer: Traditional American Melody

Scripture Reference: 1 Samuel 7:12 *"Then Samuel took a stone and set it up between Mizpah and Shen. He named it Ebenezer, saying, 'Thus far has the LORD helped us.'"* (NIV)

Isaiah 25:1 *"O LORD, you are my God; I will exalt you and praise your name, for in perfect faithfulness you have done marvelous things, things planned long ago."* (NIV)

"Come, Thou Fount of Every Blessing" reminds us to seek a relationship with Jesus every day. This hymn was written by Robert Robinson. Robinson was born September 27, 1735 in Swaffham, Norfolk, England. When he was eight years old, his father died. His mother thought it would be a good idea for Robinson to learn a trade. She sent him to London to learn barbering, but there Robinson joined a gang. One time Robinson and the rest of the gang went to a church meeting, intending to make fun of the preacher. Instead, Robinson liked what the preacher said and became a Christian. Robinson ultimately became a preacher himself but often struggled to maintain his Christian life.

Nobody knows for sure who wrote the hymn tune itself. It is a beautiful old melody that was found in a book of sacred music published by John Wyeth in 1813.

(Remember, when we refer to the "hymn" we are referring to the words. The music is called the "hymn tune").

Come, Thou Fount of Every Blessing

ROBERT ROBINSON

Traditional American Melody
Arranged by Steven V. Taylor

1st time: Solo
2nd time: Choir

1. Come Thou
(2. Here I)

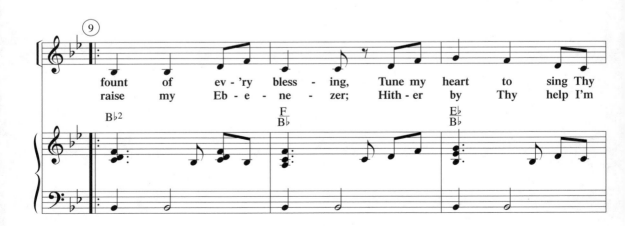

fount	of	ev - 'ry	bless - ing,	Tune my	heart	to	sing Thy
raise	my	Eb - e - ne - zer;	Hith - er	by	Thy	help I'm

72

74

Amazing Grace

Hymn writer: John Newton (1725-1807)
Composer: From *Virginia Harmony*

Scripture Reference: Ephesians 2:8-9 *"For it is by grace you have been saved, through faith– and this not from yourselves, it is the gift of God– not by works, so that no one can boast."* (NIV)

"Amazing Grace" is one of the favorite hymns of Christians throughout the world. This hymn has been sung in nearly every Christian church, and in many different languages. John Newton, who was born on July 24, 1725 in London, wrote "Amazing Grace". When Newton was only 6 years old, his mother died. He went off to sea with his father when he was eleven years old. Newton lived a life which was wild and ungodly. He became the captain of a slave ship. Newton began turning to Christ in March of 1748 while at sea. He feared his ship would be lost so he began seeking God. He did become a Christian, but still remained a slave ship captain. After trying to improve the conditions on the slave voyages, he finally became a great opponent to slavery. Newton married and moved back to London, became a minister, and lived the rest of his life preaching the gospel and fighting slavery. He was always amazed that God loved him and would use him as his servant.

"Amazing Grace" is an American folk tune. James P. Carrell and David S. Clayton published it in a book called "Virginia Harmony." "Amazing Grace" has one of the most recognizable tunes of any Christian song ever written.

(Remember, when we refer to the "hymn" we are referring to the words. The music is called the "hymn tune").

Amazing Grace

JOHN NEWTON

Virginia Harmony, 1831
Arranged by Steven V. Taylor

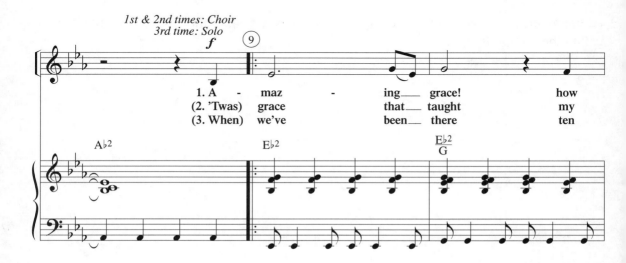

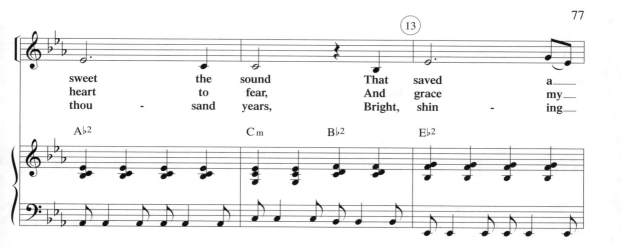

78

It Is Well with My Soul

Hymn writer: Horatio G. Spafford (1828-1888)
Composer: Philip P. Bliss (1838-1876)

Scripture Reference:Psalm 46:1 *"God is our refuge and strength, an ever-present help in trouble."* (NIV)

"It Is Well with My Soul" has one of the most inspiring hymn stories you will ever hear. Horatio G. Spafford, the writer of the lyrics, was born in North Troy, New York. As an adult, he was a successful lawyer in Chicago. He was also acquainted with many fine Christian leaders of his day. As a result of the Chicago fire of 1871, Spafford lost much of his valuable real estate. This was upsetting to his family, so he decided to take his wife and four daughters on a cruise to Great Britain. There, they could also assist D. L. Moody, a famous evangelistic preacher and his personal friend, with a revival meeting. At the last minute, Horatio himself had to stay behind due to a business emergency. He sent his family on ahead saying he would join them in a few days. His wife and four daughters sailed toward Great Britain on the Ville du Havre. While on the way, the Ville du Havre collided with an English ship, the Lochearn. The Ville du Havre sank. Horatio's wife survived, but their daughters drowned. Days later, Horatio crossed the ocean to join his wife. While crossing, he had the boat pause at the very point where the Ville du Havre had gone down and his daughters had died. He wrote the lyrics to "It is Well with My Soul" at that special place as a gift to God. It is amazing that in all his sorrow, he could write such words of encouragement and hope. Spafford and his wife eventually had two more daughters, and the family moved to Jerusalem to found a mission to serve the poor.

Philip P. Bliss heard Spafford's story and quickly set the poem to music. Philip Bliss was an accomplished writer of hymns himself. He could write lyrics as well as melodies. Many of the hymns written by Philip Bliss are still sung today.

(Remember, when we refer to the "hymn" we are referring to the words. The music is called the "hymn tune").

It Is Well with My Soul

HORATIO G. SPAFFORD

PHILIP P. BLISS
Arranged by Steven V. Taylor

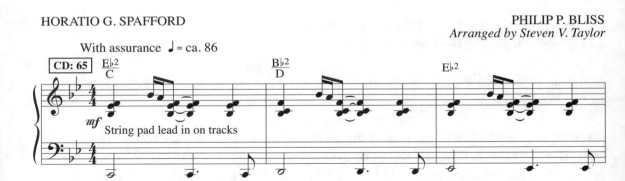

1. When peace like a
(2. And,) Lord haste the

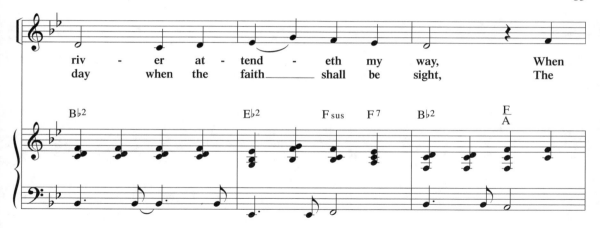

riv - er at - tend - eth my way, When
day when the faith____ shall be sight, The

Bb2   Eb2   Fsus   F7   Bb2   F/A

13

sor - rows like sea bil - lows roll,
clouds be rolled back as a scroll,

Gm7   Bb6/C   C4/2   C   Fsus

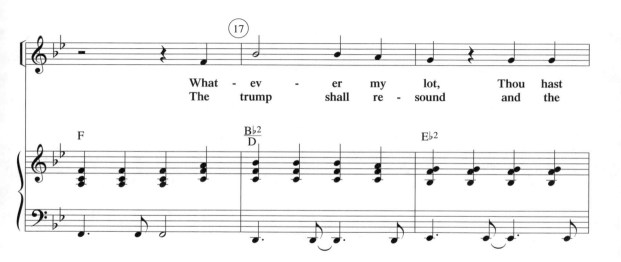

17

What - ev - er my lot, Thou hast
The trump shall re - sound and the

F   Bb2/D   Eb2

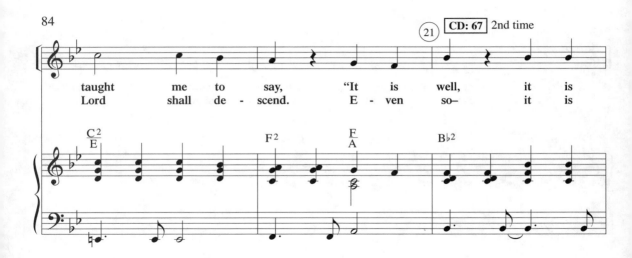

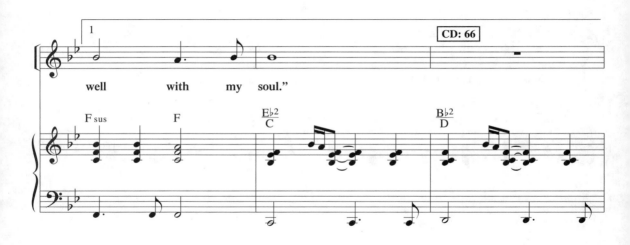

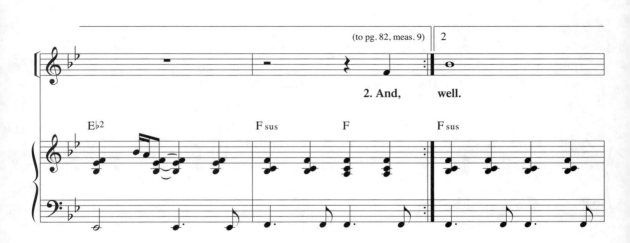

86

Rock of Ages

Hymn writer: Augustus M. Toplady (1740-1778)
Composer: Thomas Hastings (1784-1872)

Scripture Reference: 1 Corinthians 10:1 *"For I do not want you to be ignorant of the fact, brothers, that our forefathers were all under the cloud and that they all passed through the sea...and drank the same spiritual drink; for they drank from the spiritual rock that accompanied them, and that rock was Christ."* (NIV)

Exodus 33:22 *"When my glory passes by, I will put you in a cleft in the rock and cover you with my hand until I have passed by."* (NIV)

"Rock of Ages" was written by Augustus Montague Toplady. Toplady was born on November 4, 1740, in Farmham, England. His father, who was in the military, died when he was very young. Toplady attended Trinity College in Dublin, Ireland. After college, he became a respected preacher who gave powerful messages to his congregations. "Rock of Ages" was Toplady's way of reminding people of the security of the Lord. He died of tuberculosis and other physical problems at the age of 38.

Thomas Hastings was the composer of the tune for "Rock of Ages." Hastings was an accomplished church musician. He had physical problems, which he dealt with all his life. But, in spite of his health problems, he wrote hundreds of hymn tunes and lyrics.

(Remember, when we refer to the "hymn" we are referring to the words. The music is called the "hymn tune").

Rock of Ages

AUGUSTUS M. TOPLADY

THOMAS HASTINGS
Arranged by Steven V. Taylor

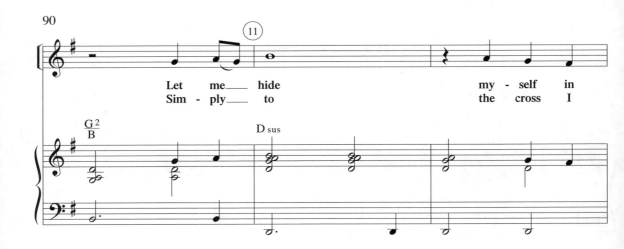

Let me___ hide my - self in
Sim - ply___ to the cross I

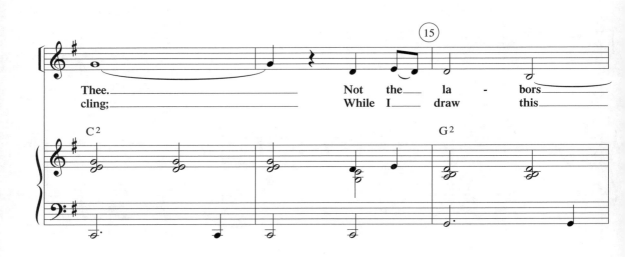

Thee._____ Not the___ la - bors___
cling;_____ While I___ draw this___

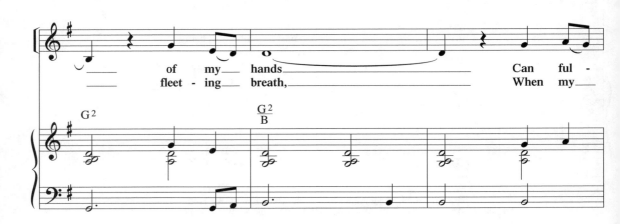

_____ of my___ hands_____ Can ful -
_____ fleet - ing___ breath,_____ When my___

CD: 73

Lord, You are___ my Rock,___ You are___ my King.

You're the King___ of___ Kings.___

King. When I___

When I soar___

soar to___ worlds un - known,

Nothing but the Blood

Hymn writer and Composer: Robert Lowry, (1826-1899)

Scripture Reference: Hebrews 9:22 *"In fact, the law requires that nearly everything be cleansed with blood, and without the shedding of blood there is no forgiveness."* (NIV)

"Nothing but the Blood" reminds us that the only way to salvation is through the blood of Jesus. This hymn is fun to sing and is a favorite of many. Robert Lowry was born March 12, 1826 in Philadelphia, Pennsylvania. He attended Bucknell University where he received a doctorate degree and became a professor of literature. He was also the pastor of the Park Avenue Baptist Church in Plainfield, New Jersey. He became the editor of the "Sunday School Songs Collections."

One of the reasons this hymn is so much fun to sing is because it was written in a question and answer style.

There are actually two more verses to this hymn.

> "Now, by this I'll overcome–
> Nothing but the blood of Jesus,
> Now, by this I'll reach my home–
> Nothing but the blood of Jesus.
>
> Glory! Glory! This I sing–
> Nothing but the blood of Jesus,
> All my praise for this I bring–
> Nothing but the blood of Jesus."

"Nothing but the Blood" was first published in the American Baptist publication in 1909. "Plainfield" was chosen as the title for the tune It was named after Plainfield, Lowry's home in New Jersey.

(Remember, when we refer to the "hymn" we are referring to the words. The music is called the "hymn tune").

Nothing but the Blood

Words and Music by
ROBERT LOWRY
Arranged by Steven V. Taylor

CD: 74

With energy ♩ = ca. 120

1. What can wash a - way my sin?
2. For my par - don___ this I see—

Noth-ing but the blood of Je - sus.___

102

All Creatures of Our God and King

Hymn writer: Francis of Assisi (1182-1226)
Composer: From *Geistliche Kirchengesange*

Scripture Reference: Psalm 145:10-11 *"All you have made will praise you, O LORD; your saints will extol you. They will tell of the glory of your kingdom and speak of your might."* (NIV)

"All Creatures of Our God and King" is a marvelous song of praise given to us by Saint Francis of Assisi. He was born in 1182 in Assisi, Italy. At the age of 25, he gave up his worldly ways and decided to devote his life to God and to the service of others, living a life of sacrifice and obedience to God Francis had a great appreciation for nature, and considered each creature as a special creation of God. "All Creatures of Our God and King" was written just before he died. This hymn reminds us that all creatures bow to God in praise.

The tune for "All Creatures of Our God and King" was found in the "English Hymnal" in 1906. This hymn has been a favorite of children's choirs for many years.

(Remember, when we refer to the "hymn" we are referring to the words. The music is called the "hymn tune").

All Creatures of Our God and King

FRANCIS OF ASSISI

Geistliche Kirchengesange
Arranged by Steven V. Taylor

106

(to pg. 104, meas. 9)

The Kids' Hymn Project Musical
by
Pam Andrews

Consider the option of creating your own mini musical with this collection of hymns. The following scripts can be combined with other dialogue to create the musical effect. Choose as many or as few sets of dialogue as you wish. You might want to add the scripture reference provided for each hymn to add another speaking part.

Dialogue for "The Solid Rock"

KID 1: Jesus, You are my Rock!
KID 2: Jesus, You are my salvation!
KID 3: Jesus, I build my life on You!
KID 4: Thank You, Jesus, for being my Rock.

Dialogue for "When I Survey the Wondrous Cross"

KID 1: Jesus paid a great price for us.
KID 2: He died on the cross for our sins.
KID 3: Then, on the third day, He arose from the dead.
KID 4: Thank You, Jesus, for the cross.

Dialogue for "Holy, Holy, Holy! Lord God Almighty"

KID 1: Jesus, You are holy.
KID 2: Jesus, You are mighty.
KID 3: Jesus, You are merciful.
KID 4: Thank You, Jesus, for blessing my life.

Dialogue for "Wonderful Words of Life"

KID 1: The Bible gives us words for life.
KID 2: The Bible gives us help.
KID 3: The Bible is the Holy Word of God.
KID 4: Thank You, Jesus, for Your Word.

Dialogue for "All Hail the Power of Jesus' Name"

KID 1: Jesus, I give You my praise!
KID 2: Jesus, I give You my worship!
KID 3: Jesus, I give You my song!
KID 4: Thank You, Jesus, for the power of Your name.

Dialogue for "Blessed Assurance"

KID 1: With Jesus in my heart, I have peace.
KID 2: With Jesus in my heart, I have joy.
KID 3: With Jesus in my heart, I have love.
KID 4: Thank You, Jesus, for your blessed assurance.

Dialogue for "I Surrender All"

KID 1: Jesus, I give You my all!
KID 2: Jesus, I give You my heart!
KID 3: Jesus, I give You my life!
KID 4: Thank You, Jesus, that I can surrender to You.

Dialogue for "My Jesus, I Love Thee"

KID 1: Jesus, You love me!
KID 2: Jesus, I love you!
KID 3: Jesus, Your love will never fail!
KID 4: Thank You, Jesus, for Your love.

Dialogue for "What a Friend We Have in Jesus"

KID 1: Jesus, You are my friend.
KID 2: Jesus, You are a friend that is true.
KID 3: Jesus, You are always there for me.
KID 4: Thank You, Jesus, for being my friend.

Dialogue for "Come, Thou Fount of Every Blessing"

KID 1: Jesus, You give me blessings.
KID 2: Jesus, You are always near.
KID 3: Jesus, you keep me safe.
KID 4: Thank You, Jesus, for all You do for me.

Dialogue for "Amazing Grace"

KID 1: Jesus, You love me as I am.
KID 2: I now see what is right because of you.
KID 3: You give me the hope of heaven.
KID 4: Thank You, Jesus, for Your amazing grace.

Dialogue for "It Is Well with My Soul"

KID 1: With Jesus, I can make it through hard times.
KID 2: With Jesus, I can walk through a storm.
KID 3: Jesus takes care of me.
KID 4: Thank You, Jesus, for all Your care.

Dialogue for "Rock of Ages"

KID 1: Jesus is my Rock!
KID 2: Jesus is my strength!
KID 3: Jesus keeps me safe in the cleft of the rock!
KID 4: Thank You, Jesus, for Your protection.

Dialogue for "Nothing but the Blood"

KID 1: Jesus shed His blood on the cross.
KID 2: His blood washes away my sins.
KID 3: I am glad Jesus lives in my heart.
KID 4: Thank You, Jesus, for washing away my sins.

Dialogue for "All Creatures of Our God and King"

KID 1: Let our voices praise the Lord!
KID 2: Let the instruments praise the Lord!
KID 3: Let all creatures praise the Lord!
KID 4: Thank You, Jesus, that we can praise You.